I Wonder Why

Mice Are Musical

and other questions about music

Josephine Paker

KINGFISHER

Kingfisher Publications Plc
New Penderel House
283–288 High Holborn
London WC1V 7HZ
www.kingfisherpub.com

First published by Kingfisher Publications Plc 1995
First published in this format 2007
10 9 8 7 6 5 4 3 2 1

1TR/0107/SHEN/RNB(RNB)/126.6MA/F

A CIP catalogue record for this book is available
from the British Library

ISBN: 978 0 7534 1457 6

Consultant: Peter Thoms
Thanks to: Waseda University, Tokyo
Illustrations: Peter Dennis (Linda Rogers); Diane
Fawcett (Artist Partners); Chris Forsey; Nick Harris
(Virgil Pomfret); Bizz Hull (Artist Partners) cover;
Tony Kenyon (B.L. Kearley) all cartoons; Nicki Palin;
Richard Ward; David Wright (Kathy Jakeman).

Printed in Taiwan

CONTENTS

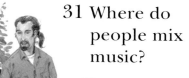

How do you sing in a round?

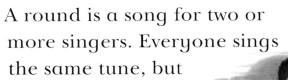

A round is a song for two or more singers. Everyone sings the same tune, but they start singing at different times. When the first singer finishes the first line, the second singer starts, and so on. One of the best-known rounds is called *Frère Jacques*.

● A round gets louder and louder as each singer joins in and softer and softer as everyone finishes their part.

● Singing can help you to learn things – your times tables, for instance. Singing makes them much easier to remember.

● People sing *Happy Birthday to You* more than any other song in the world. At first it wasn't a birthday song at all. It was called *Good Morning to All*.

4

- An opera is a musical play in which every single word is sung – even something as ordinary as "May I have a drink, please?"

Who sings in the bath?

Just about everyone loves to sing in the bath. Your voice is your own special musical instrument, which you can 'play' any time and anywhere you like. As you sing, air wobbles across stretchy ribbons in your throat, called vocal cords. We hear this vibrating air as sounds.

- Voices sound beautiful in the bath. The sounds bounce off the walls and the water to make rich, loud echoes.

Where can you find a gamelan?

A gamelan is a kind of orchestra from Indonesia. Drums, gongs, xylophones and chimes all play together to make a magical tinkling sound. There can be as many as 40 instruments in a gamelan.

● Washboards are just trays scrub clothes on. But some jc musicians play them like an instrument. They scrape a sti or thimble across the ridges.

● Gamelan players treat their instruments with great respect.

Are rattles just for babies?

It isn't only babies who like the dry, swishing sound rattles make. The first ones were probably dried plant pods, full of seeds. South American rattles called maracas are still often filled with dried beans. You could fill a yoghurt pot with some to make your own rattle.

● The triangle is one of the smallest instruments. Larger triangles are used to warn people about fire in some parts of the world, but sirens work better on noisy roads!

What roars like a bull?

The bull-roarer doesn't really roar like an angry bull! It's a block of wood fixed to a piece of string. You whirl it above your head and it makes a strange screaming noise.

Are guitar strings really made of string?

Like all musical strings, guitar strings are usually made of metal or nylon, not string! As you pluck them, the strings shake. This makes the air shake too and we hear it as sounds. It rolls around inside the hollow guitar, and makes rich notes.

- You tune a stringed instrument by turning the pegs at the end of its nec Tightening a string make a higher note. Loosening it makes a lower one.

- Stringed instruments come in all shapes and sizes. This old lute was made using the hard skin of an armadillo!

What's double about a double bass?

The double bass got its name because it used to 'double', or copy, the cello. 'Bass' means low, and the double bass *does* have a deep voice! Pluck one of its thick strings and it makes a very low note.

● Niccolo Paganini was a genius on the violin. He could play it behind his back, upside-down, and with a blindfold on!

How do you learn the sitar?

The sitar is one of the most difficult stringed instruments to play. To learn it, you have to watch and listen to a skilled player. Players learn groups of notes called ragas, and then put them together to make beautiful, haunting music.

● The Indian vina balances comfortably on the shoulder as the player plucks the strings.

Why do flutes have holes?

To play the flute, you blow over the blowhole. The air shakes its way down the tube and you hear it come out as a musical sound. You change notes by covering and uncovering the different holes of the flute with your fingers.

● Penny whistles belong to the same family of musical instruments as flutes – the woodwind family. You play the penny whistle like a recorder, by blowing into the mouthpiece, and covering the holes.

● Panpipes are named after an ancient Greek god called Pan, who was half-goat. He cut some reeds of different lengths, tied them together, and blew across the top.

When is a serpent not a serpent?

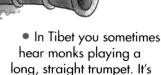

When it's a woodwind instrument! It's easy to see how the serpent got its snaky name – it's so curly! It was invented 400 years ago, but isn't played much these days.

Snakes are deaf, but they sway in time with a snake-charmer's music. They're keeping their eyes on the pipe, in case it's an enemy snake!

● In Tibet you sometimes hear monks playing a long, straight trumpet. It's so heavy that the far end has to be held up as the monk plays.

How do you stretch brass?

The trombone is one brass instrument that needs stretching. It has a long, sliding arm. The trombonist moves this slide in and out to make the different notes.

15

Who sits where in an orchestra?

The players in an orchestra all have their own place to sit. It depends on which instrument they play, and to which 'family' the instrument belongs. Violins, cellos and other stringed instruments all sit together at the front and the noisier brass and woodwind instruments are at the back.

● Johann Strauss conducte a vast orchestra in 1872. There were nearly 1,000 players, with over 400 people playing the violin.

● The French composer Jean-Baptiste Lully used to conduct by banging a big stick on the floor. One day, he missed and banged his own foot instead! Ouch!

Piano

Harp

French horr

D

Percussion

Tuba

Trombones

Bassoon

Double basses

Trumpets

Oboes

Cellos

Flutes

Violins

● The conductor is the boss.
He or she tells the musicians
when to play, how loudly to
play, how fast, and – of
course – when to stop!

Who writes music?

People who write music are called composers. They write down musical notes just as you write down words. Music isn't always written down though. Some people learn how to play a piece of music by simply copying a teacher or something they have heard.

● Many composers don't write down their ideas on paper any more. They key in the notes on a computer and can immediately play back what they have written.

Which five-year-old composed music?

Wolfgang Amadeus Mozart was a musical genius. At the age of five, he composed his very first piece of music. By the time he died, aged only thirty-five, he had written over 600 works.

● Mozart was one of the greatest – and youngest – composers. His father took him on a tour of Europe to show him off.

Which composer was deaf?

The German composer Ludwig van Beethoven slowly became deaf. At first he used a curly ear trumpet to help him to hear, but it was no use. Soon he was composing music in his head that he was never able to hear.

● Musical notes are written on a set of five lines called a stave. A high note is written high up on the stave. The shape of the note, and whether it's black or white, shows how long it should last.

● Music isn't always written down. Jazz musicians often make up the music as they go along. This is called a 'jam session'.

Which is the biggest instrument?

The organ is the biggest musical instrument. Organ music can make the windows rattle! The largest and loudest organ in the world is in Atlantic City, America. It's so huge that it sounds as loud as 25 brass bands playing together! It has 12 keyboards and over 33,000 pipes. Sadly this record-breaking instrument doesn't work very well these days.

● The Russian composer Sergei Rachmaninov had enormous hands. He could stretch over 12 keys on the piano – that's probably twice as far as you could manage.

What's the longest piece of music ever played?

It takes all day and half the night to listen to a performance of Erik Satie's *Vexations*. This is because the piece has to be played 840 times. It needs six pianists to take turns with the playing. Just one might fall asleep!

• This enormous guitar in Bristol, England is so huge that you can climb inside it. If you twang its strings the noise is deafening!

Which is the most valuable instrument?

Three hundred years ago, an Italian called Antonio Stradivari made the most wonderful violins. His instruments are now so rare and so valuable that they cost a fortune – far more than the price of a house!

Who tells stories by dancing?

Ballet is a way of telling a story through music and dance. The sound of the music and the movements of the dancers tell you what's going on as clearly as any story in a book. And, of course, it's beautiful to watch and to hear.

• Sometimes a story is turned into a ballet – *The Tales of Beatrix Potter* for instance.

• Some street performers are more like gymnasts than dancers! They do daring handstands, somersaults and leaps.

What's the dance of the spider?

An Italian dance, called the tarantella, is named after the tarantula spider. People used to think that if someone was bitten by this deadly spider, they would only be cured by dancing the wild dance of the tarantella. As the dancer twisted and leapt, all of the on-lookers beat time with tambourines and castanets.

● The lowest a limbo dancer has ever limboed is under a flaming wooden bar just 10 centimetres off the ground – that's less than the height of this book!

● When you dance the conga, you hold the person in front by the waist and dance along in a line. The longest-ever conga stretched the length of 500 ice rinks and was made up of 120,000 people.

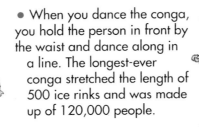

Whose singing wrecked ships?

In fairy tales, mermaids were magical creatures – half-women and half-fish – who lived in the sea near dangerous, rocky coasts. They sang so sweetly that any sailors who heard them forgot everything else – including how to steer their ship.

● In the Ancient Greek myth, Orpheus played his lyre so beautifully that he persuaded the god of the underworld to free his wife, Eurydice. But then he broke a promise not to look back at her and lost her after all.

● People used to blame shipwrecks on mermaids. They thought their singi lured sailors and their ships onto the jagged rock

● Saint Cecilia is the patron saint of music. In pictures of her, she usually has a miniature organ on her lap.

● In a tale by Hans Andersen, a Chinese emperor loved to listen to a nightingale's song. When the bird flew away, the emperor missed its music so much that he had a mechanical model made in its place.

Who played a magic pipe?

In the story of the Pied Piper, a man with a magic pipe enchants the children of Hamelin in Germany. When he plays, they follow him out of town – never to return.

Which frog sings?

Male frogs love to sing. They puff out their throat to make a big space where the air can vibrate, and the concert begins. Frogs sing surprisingly loudly, but it's not everyone's idea of music!

● The composer Domenico Scarlatti wrote a piece that is nicknamed *Cat's Fugue*. Scarlatti said that his cat made up the tune as it tiptoed along the keys of his harpsichord!

Why are mice musical?

The male grasshopper mouse of North America uses his shrill chirruping song to attract a mate. He stands up on his back legs and sings his heart out. It' his way of telling all the female mice around what a fine, strong mouse he is.

Who sings the dawn chorus?

As the Sun rises on spring and summer mornings, the birds wake up and start to twitter. This makes a beautiful dawn chorus. Some songs warn others to keep away – others tell a mate where to find some tasty food.

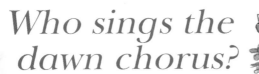

- Each bird has its own special song, unlike any other's. Birds recognise each other by their song, just as we recognise friends by their voice.

Who sings under water?

Humpback whales seem to sing to each other under the ocean. Some scientists think the whales are singing about where they've swum and what they've been doing. No other animal's song lasts as long as the humpback whale's, and it can be heard hundreds of kilometres away.

- Elephants sometimes use their trunk like a musical instrument. They blow through it and make a tremendous trumpeting noise.

How do termites help to make music?

The didgeridoo is a long, musical pipe from Australia. It's made from a log of the eucalyptus tree, which is buried inside a termites' mound. The wood-eating termites gnaw away at the soft wood inside the log, leaving a hollow pipe. Then the pipe is decorated. These days, some didgeridoos are hollowed out by hand, but they don't give the same rich sound.

Which harp fits inside your mouth?

The tiny Jew's harp doesn't look like a proper harp. You put it between your teeth, and twang its metal tongue with your finger. It makes your lips feel funny because the metal vibrates so much.

● Didgeridoo-players can breathe in at the same time as they're blowing out through their instrument.

• The Masai people of Kenya play an instrument called a thumb piano. It has metal strips which you pluck with your thumb.

Which instrument is made with a spider's web?

If you take a cow's horn, make a little hole at the pointed end, and cover the wide end with a tough kind of spider's web, you've got a mirliton. Mirlitons are played in Africa. They make a buzzy sound when you blow or sing through them.

• An American jazz musician called Roland Kirk could play three saxophones all at once! He must have had lots of puff!

• Not all bagpipes come from Scotland. This African goatskin bagpipe has been decorated with a carved wooden goat's head!

Can a robot play the piano?

A clever Japanese robot called WABOT-2 can whizz its fingers over a keyboard much faster than a human can. It can either read new music, or choose a song it has played before and stored in its memory. The cleverest thing about WABOT-2 is its sensitive fingers. It can play gently or furiously.

● WABOT-2's head is like a camcorder. As the robot reads music, the camera 'films' what it sees and stores it in its memory to play again.

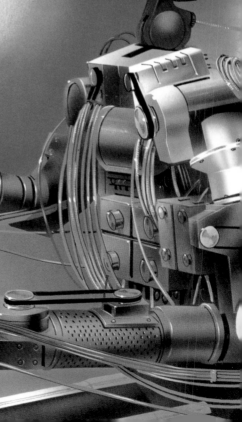

Where do people mix music?

In a recording studio, the voices and instruments are recorded separately. The producer mixes the parts together on a machine called a mixing desk. He or she checks the sounds are balanced and every part can be heard clearly.

● Drum machines make the sound of all sorts of drums – but they're only as big as a chocolate box. Some of them have pads to tap out your rhythm on.

● You can record any sound you like on a sampler – even a dog's bark. You put the sounds you've sampled into tunes as if they were musical notes.

Can you be an entire orchestra?

Synthesisers are machines that can make the sound of every instrument in the orchestra. One minute they sound like a flute, the next they sound like a violin. They'll even play a simple drum pattern to give your music a beat.

Index

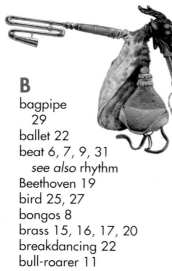